# MISUNDERSTOOD
## A BIG BROTHER'S JOURNEY

By: Jenelle Simpson
Rushawn Evans and
Latyah Evans

Illustrated By:
Katie African

Copyright © 2023 by Jenelle Simpson, Rushawn Evans, and Laiyah Evans

All rights reserved.

No part of this publication may be reproduced, distributed, or transmitted in any form or by any means, including photocopying, recording, or other electronic or mechanical methods, without the prior written permission of the publishers. For permission requests, contact Jenelle Simpson at info@jenellesimpson.com.

Book Cover by Katie African

Illustrations by Katie African

Published by Roots of Jenerational Legacy

ISBN 978-1-7779875-6-5 (paperback)
ISBN 978-1-7779875-7-2 (e-book)

www.jenellesimpson.com

Our first children's book is dedicated to our late grandma and
Great-grandma Jasmine Rose Thomas, better known as sweetie.

Grandma sweetie, you poured into us, and we are extremely
blessed to have had you as our mama and now
our guardian angel. Thank you for teaching and demonstrating to
us how to live, laugh, smile, love, forgive, pray, and live as one.
Your teachings and lessons we will carry with us forever.

To all the children in the world learning to understand, love
and navigate through life, never stop believing in yourselves
and being the utmost best for yourself. Sky is not the limit!

Our dad, our mommy, our uncle, our aunts,
our grandma, grandpa and to each other, thanks for
believing in us and pushing us to be and always do more.

**"You are phenomenally created in your own perfect image, own it and walk tall."**
– Rushawn and Laiyah Evans

I remember when I wanted a sibling, specifically a little sister. I'd ask Mom and Dad to go to the store and buy me a sibling, as if it were something you could just walk into a store and pick up off a shelf. Every time we went to my favorite store, Walmart (I bet it's your favorite store too), I had the biggest smile on my face, hopeful that we'd find a chunky baby sister for me.

I quickly realized that getting a sibling wouldn't be as easy as I'd imagined when Mom finally got pregnant. Her belly looked like a big balloon, and she waddled like a duck. Her belly was perfectly round, but I always wondered how she carried all that baby! Moms are strong! My mom is tough, determined, and always gets things done.

Hey, before we continue, I almost forgot to introduce myself! My name is Rushawn, Rushawn Devonne Evans, and I'm eight years old. I'm a young man now. I even have some changes in my voice… Mom says it's just squeaks from the weather change, but it's bass. Trust me.

Many people have said I look like Will Smith because my ears are big and flare out just like his, but my mom says I'm unique, special, and born for greatness. That's why God gave me special ears for my special talent. These are 'millionaire' ears!

It took me a very long time to get comfortable with my ears and accept the fact that I'm different. Some people may make silly and not so nice comments about my ears, such as calling me 'dumbo' and monkey', but I have a great support system that encourages me to embrace my 'millionaire' ears.

Oh! And did I mention they call me 'big foot' because my feet are bigger than most children's my age? I get my feet from my dad. In case you were wondering, I wear a size eight to eight and half in men's shoes. So there you have it. 'Big foot' it is!

My height? Yes, I'm tall too, but they don't call me 'the gentle giant'. Hmm, I wonder why.

Mom and Dad gave me the name 'star boy', said I was truly God sent, and I turned Mom's heart upside down. But I used to be a hyper toddler. When mom was pregnant with my sister, I didn't make it easy for her. I was going through my terrible threes stage. I always wondered what that meant, so I did a little research. It's the stage when children start to change their behavior, throw unexplained terrible tantrums, and become less controllable.

That was me. Less controllable and more 'I want what I want'.

I used to throw myself on the floor and bang my head on the floor whenever I didn't get my way. Mom was so concerned that something bad was going to happen to me, so she had to make sure that I didn't have any underlying conditions, such as ADHD (attention deficit hyperactivity disorder). ADHD is a condition that affects people's behaviour. People with ADHD can seem restless, may have trouble concentrating, and may act impulsively.

Mom said ADHD is quite common, and it's not a terrible thing. It certainly didn't mean I was a bad child, but my impulsive and spontaneous behaviour concerned her. Some days, she cried about it.

Eventually, she took me to see my favorite doctor, Dr. Morris, to get advice on what to do. After that visit, I questioned why Dr. Morris was my favorite doctor because he told Mom to take away all my favorite things, including my toys and TV shows, whenever I had an episode and threw temper tantrums.

This was supposed to help me learn to think before I acted. Guess what? Mom said it worked!

Oh! And Dr. Morris is still my favorite doctor because he has all these delicious lollipops that I get a handful of every visit... So there's no hard feelings at all!

He was just doing his job.

Mom and I were BFFs (Best Friends Forever), and we still are, but our relationship is a bit different now. We used to do everything together and people called me her 'handbag' because I used to always be wrapped in her arms like a purse. We had movie dates, park dates, dinner dates, and late-night cackling. Oh, and my sushi Fridays. We'd go to the Scarborough Town Centre Mall to buy avocado and cucumber rolls… Oh, and Kernels caramel popcorn.

Those were the good old days! The days before my sibling arrived.

I clearly didn't get the memo about the sweet and sour parts of having a sibling. You know those keyring candies? They're sour when you first take a bite and then you keep chewing to get to the sweet parts. That's what having a sibling is like. I wish I'd known the beloved sibling I'd begged for would rock my world.

Life was a breeze before Laiyah Shoniah, my sister, arrived. I was so excited that I'd sing songs and watch Elmo with her when she was in Mom's tummy. Elmo was one of my favorite cartoon shows. I cleaned my room everyday, waiting for her arrival.

Shopping for her was the best part because whenever Mom bought her a little summin', she got summin' for me too. Beyblades were my favorite, and I had a ton. A baby on the way was a blessing in disguise because I was extra spoiled. I had no complaints about that.

Oh, and the hospital visits to see the baby in 3D were epic. I had a lot of questions, like how did the baby get there? How does it eat? How does it survive? How does it breathe? Just wow!

The feeling of becoming a big brother made me bubble on the inside. Soon, there would be a little person who'd admire me! I just knew I was going to be a great big brother. I'd kiss her chubby cheeks, we'd play all day… and I'd boss her around. But don't tell Mom I said that.

Five years later, I now wonder what the bananas I was thinking when I pleaded for a sister.

I chose Laiyah's name because I wanted her to become a singer one day. I thought it would be a perfect stage name. "Welcome to the stage, four-time award-winning song writer and artist, Laiyah Shoniah Evans!" That sounds catchy, right?

I was right. She can sing her heart out, but she's so shy!

I always try to push her out of her comfort zone and remind her of how beautiful and talented she is.

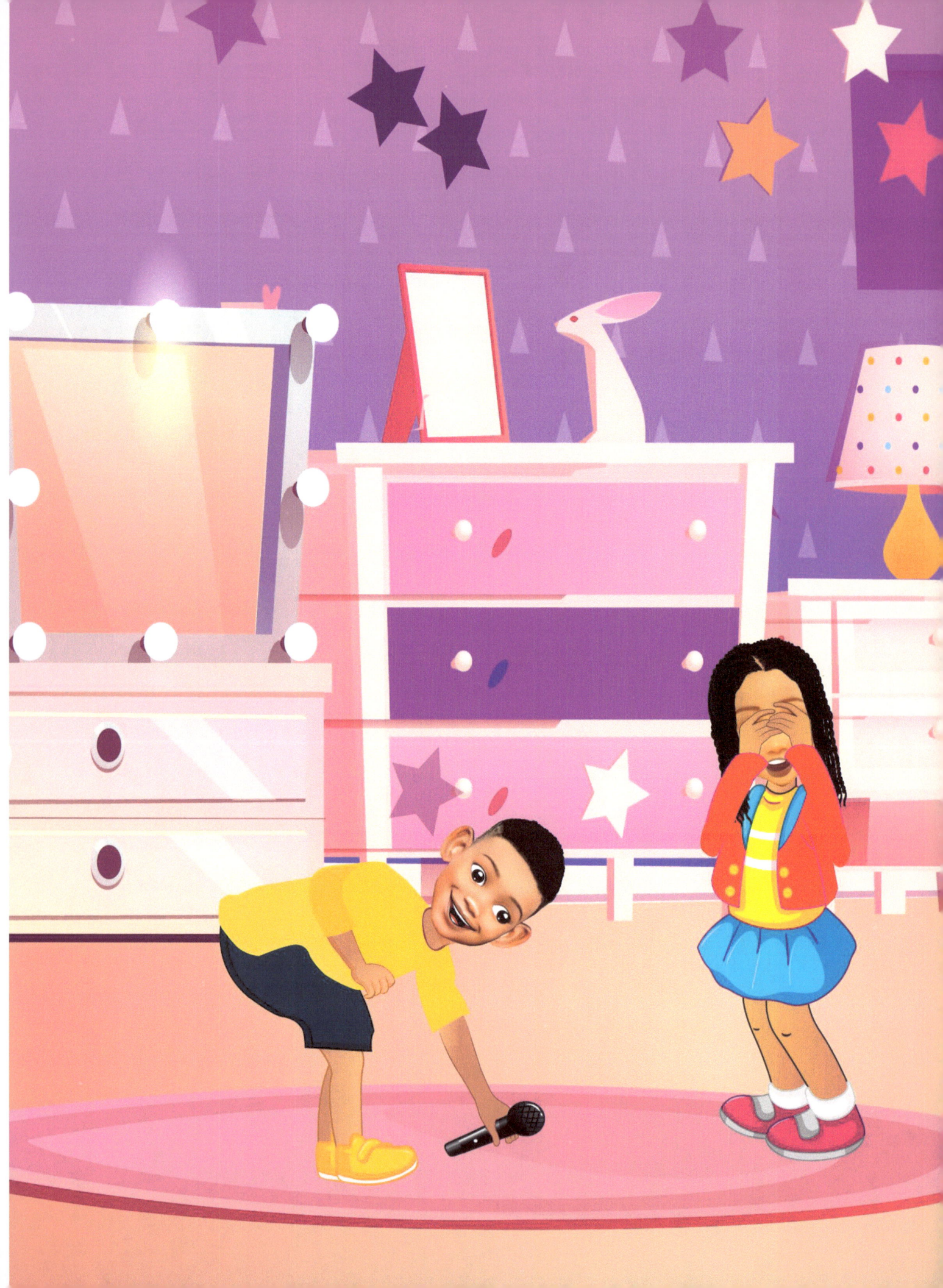

Not only can she sing, but she screams. She's always screaming at me with some added spice!

I thought I was going to be the one bossing her around, but she assured me she was the boss.

Mom says we fight a lot because we're the same horoscope sign. We're both Leos and our birthdays are a week apart... CAN YOU IMAGINE?

Mom loves to say, "God knew what he was doing when he gave me two Leos." And then she looks up at the sky and smiles before saying, " Thank you, Lord."

What is she thanking God for? Laiyah and I fight all the time.

Leos are lions and we're a fire sign. We're compassionate, big-hearted, self-assured, and natural leaders. Mom always tells us we're naturally strong, brave-hearted, competitive, and born to dominate in any and everything we set out to do. She expresses how powerful we are and says our signs soar through us. But most importantly, we should always love and take care of each other no matter what.

Laiyah and I fight hard, but Mom's right. We love even harder.

When Laiyah and I fight, it breaks Mom's heart and she gets mad. She asks, "What if something unexpectedly happened to one of you? What would you do? You should always think before you speak. Calm down and act with love first and always."

I feel guilty arguing with Laiyah, and I'm always the first to apologize because that's what older siblings do.

When Laiyah was younger, I didn't want to leave her at home and go to school. I couldn't wait to go home and see her. Now, we tend to push each other's buttons and debate on who gets the last word, and she takes the trophy every time!

But that's okay. We're human. We go through things and we make up.

As Laiyah gets older, I'm more protective of her. Mom and Dad expect me to always be on the lookout for her.

Sometimes I used to get frustrated having to always share things with her, such as my favorite food, my toys, and my friends. I quickly got fed up and just wanted to do my own thing. If anything happened to her, you'd hear, "Rushawn, what happened?" And it was automatically my fault. "You're the older one, so I expect better," my parents would say.

Why is everything me?

The answer is simple. It's because I asked for a sibling and pop... here she is. She admires me, and I'm supposed to love, respect, and set examples for her.

When I was her age, I wasn't perfect.

We go through various stages in life, and she's going through hers. We're different people, and we have different personalities. We won't always get along, but that doesn't mean we don't love each other.

Since I turned eight, Mom and Dad decided that the burden on me was a little too much. They asked me if there was anything they were doing that Laiyah and I didn't like. Was there anything they could improve on as parents?

OH, BOY! Was I glad they asked that question. Just like that, communication was the resolution!

I still look out for Laiyah and guard her with my heart, but we do our own separate things, and I no longer get in trouble when she does something wrong because Laiyah is older and knows better.

I misunderstood the responsibilities and requirements of being an older sibling and older brother. I thought it was going to be a breeze and endless fun. I thought I could boss her around a bit… But my Laiyah isn't a push over. She's extra sweet on the inside with a tough exterior. And she has an overly protective brother… me!

Life with a sibling won't always be easy. You'll fight, scream, cry, be treated unfairly sometimes, and things may change around the house a bit. But it's the best feeling to have a sibling as a best friend, an extra person to love.

# SIBLING PLEDGE

1. I will do my best not to get frustrated with my sibling.
2. I will always try to be understanding towards my sibling.
3. I will always act with compassion.
4. I will learn to use my words and communicate to my full and best capability when I do not like something my sibling does.
5. I will always maintain a healthy and respectful relationship with my sibling.
6. I will respect my sibling's boundaries and personal space.
7. I will always love my sibling.
8. I will clean my sibling's room if I make a mess.
9. I will clean up after myself and not expect my sibling to do it because they are older.
10. I will not enter my sibling's room without permission.
11. I will finish all my chores and not leave bits and pieces for my siblings to finish.
12. I will always be nice.
13. I will share with my sibling.
14. I will not be selfish.
15. I will always buy my sibling treats and bring back goodies when they are not out with me.
16. I will follow this sibling pledge.

# YOUR SIBLING PLEDGE

## Create your own personalized sibling pledge

www.ingramcontent.com/pod-product-compliance
Lightning Source LLC
Chambersburg PA
CBHW050739110526
44590CB00002B/28